MOO The Cow-tastrophe
(As It Was and So It Is)

Written and Illustrated by Bobbi Thies

Copyright © 2017 by Bobbi Thies

All rights reserved. This book or any portion thereof may not be reproduced or used in any manner whatsoever without the express written permission of the publisher except for the use of brief quotations in a book review.

ISBN 978-0-692-93363-3

First Printing, 2017
Printed in the United States of America

Illustrations by Bobbi Thies
Cover Illustration Copyright © 2017 by Bobbi Thies

Bobbi Thies
Milford, Ohio 45150
www.bobbithies.com

The morning at the barn started in a quiet way. The horses were being fed and others led to the exercise paddocks.

I was standing at the front door waving good-bye to a few children who had just finished their riding lessons.

Suddenly the garbage truck pulled up the driveway with a large black and white cow following close behind.

The driver jumped out of the truck and asked, "Do you know where this cow lives? It's been following me. I think it's lost."

"I'm not sure I know where it lives," I answered, "but I remember hearing a cow moo when I've ridden my horse in the field. Perhaps it lives on the other side of the road."

The man got back in his truck and started driving away. The cow followed the truck and I followed the cow, hoping to chase it home. Instead the cow ran across the road and behind the houses.

Two miniature dachshunds came running toward me, barking the whole way. A lady appeared at the door.

"Do you own a cow?" I asked.

"Oh yes," she said. "We have a cow named MOO."

"Well I think your cow is loose."

"Oh no, MOO is loose," said the lady, putting her hand up to her mouth. "How will I ever get her back in the pasture?" Coming out of her house she said, "maybe if we get a bucket, MOO will see me and think I'm going to feed her."

MOO had been running behind the houses. Suddenly when she saw the lady pick up the bucket, she ran toward us.

MOO came up so quickly that she knocked the lady down. "Oh my," said the lady. "I think I need help getting up."

I felt my face redden as I grabbed MOO's horns and held her until the lady could roll away and pull herself up onto a nearby bench. "That's not nice! You stop that," I said to MOO.

MOO was so excited to be back home that she ran behind the bench and put her front feet on the lady's shoulders to give her a hug. But MOO was too big; she knocked the lady off the bench and to the ground.

There was a small green shed nearby and I asked the lady if she thought she could run to the shed. "Yes I can," she said. The lady made it safely inside and watched me through a window in the door.

I turned toward MOO and noticed her hoof was caught in the slats of the bench. Before I could help her, she got her foot out!

The lady called me to get some of MOO's grain out of the green garbage can. "Maybe she'll follow you into the pasture, if she sees you put the food in her feed box." I called back, "okay, but where's the green garbage can?"

"By the pheasant pen, next to the chicken coop, across from the pot bellied pig," shouted the lady.

𝕸𝕺𝕺 watched me the whole time as I walked toward the garbage can, opened it and put a handful of grain in the bucket. As soon as I shook the bucket and headed toward the pasture, 𝕸𝕺𝕺 started to follow.

When I opened the gate, five goats rushed out. "Oh, I'm so sorry I let your goats out." I said to the lady.

"Don't worry," she said, "they won't run away."

However when the goats ran out, MOO stopped following me. The lady called to me to open the other gate to the pasture and put MOO's grain in her feed box.

This time MOO followed me through the gate into the pasture. I put the grain in her feed box, ran out and closed the gate behind me. The lady came out of the shed, as I closed the other gate. MOO was safe again!

"Oh thank you for helping me get MOO in the pasture," the lady said. "I don't know what I would have done if MOO was lost."

As we talked, MOO turned and looked at us as if to say she was glad to be home.

Milton Keynes UK
Ingram Content Group UK Ltd.
UKHW051248220124
436338UK00010B/39